READING POWER

Famous American Trails

The Oregon Trail

From Independence, Missouri, to Oregon City, Oregon

Arlan Dean

The Rosen Publishing Group's
PowerKids Press™
New York

Published in 2003 by The Rosen Publishing Group, Inc.
29 East 21st Street, New York, NY 10010

First Edition

Book Design: Christopher Logan

Photo Credits: Cover courtesy Utah Historical Society; pp. 4–5, 6–7 Denver Public Library, Western History Collection, images X-21874, WHJ-10180; p. 5 (inset) Christopher Logan; pp. 7 (inset), 18–19 © Hulton/Archive/Getty Images; p. 8 Oregon Historical Society, (left) OrHi 5922, (right) OrHi 1645; p. 9 Northwest Museum of Arts & Culture/Eastern Washington State Historical Society, Spokane, Washington, L95-24.72, Lee Moorhouse; pp. 10–11 Currier & Ives, "The Rocky Mountains—Emigrants Crossing the Plains," 1866, 56.300.40, courtesy Museum of the City of New York; pp. 12–13 © David Muench/Corbis; p. 13 (inset) State Archives of Michigan; pp. 14–15 © North Wind Picture Archives; p. 15 (inset) © Layne Kennedy/Corbis; p. 17 Milstein Division of Local History, United States History and Genealogy, The New York Public Library, Astor, Lenox and Tilden Foundations; p. 19 (inset) © Bohemian Nomad Picturemakers/Corbis; p. 20 Still Picture Branch, National Archives and Records Administration; p. 21 © Bill Moeller

Library of Congress Cataloging-in-Publication Data

Dean, Arlan.
The Oregon Trail : from Independence, Missouri to Oregon City, Oregon / Arlan Dean.
    p. cm. — (Famous American trails)
Summary: Describes the Oregon Trail and the pioneers who settled in the Pacific Northwest.
Includes bibliographical references and index.
ISBN 0-8239-6478-7 (lib. bdg.)
1. Oregon National Historic Trail—Juvenile literature. 2. Overland journeys to the Pacific—Juvenile literature. 3. Pioneers—West (U.S.)—History—19th century—Juvenile literature. 4. Frontier and pioneer life—West (U.S.)—Juvenile literature. 5. Frontier and pioneer life—Oregon—Juvenile literature. [1. Oregon National Historic Trail. 2. Overland journeys to the Pacific. 3. Pioneers. 4. Frontier and pioneer life—West (U.S.) 5. West (U.S.)—History.] I. Title.
F597 .D43 2003
978'.02—dc21
                                        2002000130

Contents

A Path West

In the 1800s, thousands of people traveled west across America. These pioneers were looking to start new lives. Many of them traveled along a path called the Oregon Trail.

Starting in Missouri, the Oregon Trail went about 2,000 miles through the present-day states of Missouri, Kansas, Nebraska, Wyoming, Idaho, and Oregon.

THE OREGON TRAIL

Legend:
- Oregon Trail
- ● Town
- ♨ Fort
- ♨ Pass

Many people packed everything they owned into wagons and traveled west on the Oregon Trail.

5

Parts of the Oregon Trail existed long before the pioneers traveled west. For hundreds of years, Native Americans used footpaths along the mountains and rivers leading west. Fur trappers and traders later connected the many footpaths to make the Oregon Trail.

This picture shows people on the Oregon Trail near the Platte River.

Some Native Americans and pioneers traded at camps near the Platte River.

Early Trail Pioneers

In 1836, Dr. Marcus Whitman led a small group of people along the Oregon Trail from Liberty, Missouri, to the Oregon Country. Soon, more people wanted to make the trip west, hoping to find a better life. By about 1840, small groups of people were using the trail.

Dr. Marcus Whitman and his wife, Narcissa, traveled the Oregon Trail in 1836.

Many Native Americans lived on the land that became the Oregon Trail.

In 1843, Jesse Applegate, a Missouri farmer, led the first big wagon train from Independence, Missouri, to the Oregon Country.

Strong oxen pulled heavy wagons to the West.

The wagon train had about 1,000 men, women, and children. About 120 wagons made up the train. The pioneers took about 5,000 oxen, horses, and cows with them.

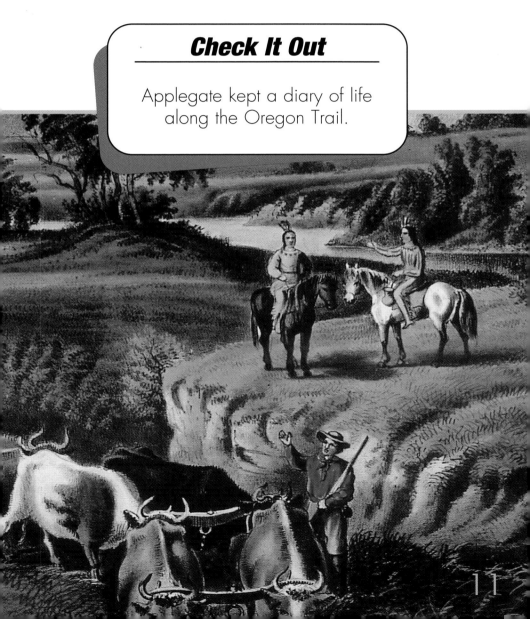

Check It Out

Applegate kept a diary of life along the Oregon Trail.

11

On the Trail

The journey west on the Oregon Trail usually took six months. The trail crossed many different kinds of land.

Check It Out

Pioneers had to cross the Rocky Mountains to reach Oregon Country. In 1812, Robert Stuart discovered a quick passageway through the mountains. It was called the South Pass.

The South Pass

In the east, pioneers crossed prairies. Farther west, they had to move their heavy wagons across unsafe rivers, like the Platte River. The pioneers also had to cross snow-covered mountains.

Robert Stuart

Trail Trouble

The pioneers faced many problems on their journey. There was often not enough food to eat. Terrible sicknesses killed many travelers. The weather went from very hot in the deserts to very cold in the mountains.

Check It Out

It is believed that over 34,000 pioneers died and were buried along the Oregon Trail.

Thunderstorms on the plains during the summer made many pioneers afraid.

Snowstorms in the mountains could trap travelers.

There were very few places along the trail where the pioneers could buy supplies. Almost everything a family needed for the trip had to be packed in their wagon.

Check It Out

Most wagons were about 12 feet long and 4 feet wide.

"From six to seven o'clock is a busy time; breakfast is to be eaten, the tents [are taken down], the wagons loaded. . . .

"All know then, at seven o'clock, the signal to march sounds, that those not ready to take their proper places in the line of march must fall into the dusty rear for the day."
—Jesse Applegate, 1843

Oxen pulling the wagon were strong, but slow. Pioneers traveled only about 15 miles a day.

Wagons were built so they could float. It was difficult to float a wagon across a river. Many wagons were caught in currents and tipped over.

The End of the Trail

Fort Laramie was a fur-trading outpost in present-day Wyoming. By 1850, about 40,000 people and 9,000 wagons had passed through the fort on the way west.

Check It Out

From around 1841 to 1861, about 300,000 people traveled the Oregon Trail.

In Oregon, pioneers found rich farmland at the end of their long journey.

Fort Laramie was a welcomed sight for travelers heading west. Here, pioneers could stock up on food and supplies.

19

Some people traveling west still used the trail even after the Transcontinental Railroad was built in 1869. Though they met great dangers on their trip, these people continued to travel the Oregon Trail to find better lives.

Once the Transcontinental Railroad was built, most people rode the train to go west. The trip on the railroad was faster and safer than using the Oregon Trail.

In 1978, the U.S. government made the Oregon Trail part of its National Trail System. The Oregon Trail played a very important part in the history of the United States.

Parts of the trail, like this one in Oregon, can still be seen today.

The Oregon Trail Time Line

1812	Robert Stuart discovers the South Pass in the Rocky Mountains.
1836	Dr. Marcus Whitman leads a small group to the Oregon Country.
1843	Jesse Applegate and about 1,000 pioneers head for Oregon.
1869	The Transcontinental Railroad is completed.
1978	The U.S. government makes the Oregon Trail part of its National Trail System.

Glossary

journey (**jehr**-nee) a long trip from one place to another

outpost (**out**-pohst) a place set up far away from any town or city to stop surprise enemy attacks or to be used as a rest stop for travelers

pass (**pas**) a low place in a mountain range

pioneers (py-uh-**nihrz**) people who go first to prepare a way for other people

plains (**playnz**) large, flat areas of land without trees

prairies (**prehr**-eez) large, flat areas of land covered in tall grass

Transcontinental Railroad (tran-skahn-tuh-**nehn**-tehl **rayl**-rohd) a railroad system going across North America

wagon train (**wag**-uhn **trayn**) a group of wagons traveling overland on a path

Resources

Books

The Oregon Trail
by Richard Conrad Stein
Children's Press (1994)

A Frontier Fort on the Oregon Trail
by Scott Steedman
McGraw-Hill Children's Publishing (1994)

Web Sites

Due to the changing nature of Internet links, PowerKids Press has developed an on-line list of Web sites related to the subjects of this book. This site is updated regularly. Please use this link to access the list:

http://www.powerkidslinks.com/fat/oret/

Index

A
Applegate, Jesse,
 10–11, 16, 21

F
Fort Laramie, 5, 18–19

J
journey, 12, 14

N
Native Americans,
 6–7, 9

O
outpost, 18
oxen, 10–11, 17

P
pioneers, 4, 6–7,
 11–17, 19, 21
Platte River, 5–7, 13
prairies, 13

T
Transcontinental
 Railroad, 20–21

W
wagon train, 10–11
Whitman, Marcus,
 8, 21

Word Count: 487

Note to Librarians, Teachers, and Parents
   If reading is a challenge, Reading Power is a solution! Reading Power
is perfect for readers who want high-interest subject matter at an accessible reading
level. These fact-filled, photo-illustrated books are designed for readers who want
straightforward vocabulary, engaging topics, and a manageable reading experience.
With clear picture/text correspondence, leveled Reading Power books put the reader
in charge. Now readers have the power to get the information they want and the skills
they need in a user-friendly format.